# THE POP-UP BOOK OF INVASIONS

# the POP-UP BOOK of INVASIONS

FIONA FARRELL

AUCKLAND UNIVERSITY PRESS

*For Doug, Ursula and Susannah, as always.*
*And for Robyn Carrig and the Rathcoola*
*Residency, with thanks and affection*

First published 2007

Auckland University Press
University of Auckland
Private Bag 92019
Auckland
New Zealand
www.auckland.ac.nz/aup

© Fiona Farrell, 2007

ISBN 978 1 86940 388 1

Publication is kindly assisted by

National Library of New Zealand Cataloguing-in-Publication Data
Farrell, Fiona, 1947-
Pop-up book of invasions / Fiona Farrell.
ISBN 978-1-869403-881
1. Title.
NZ821.2—dc 22

Cover design: Sarah Maxey
Printed by Astra Print Ltd, Wellington

Ireland. Whatever is asked of me,
I know pleasantly.
Every taking that took her
from the beginning of the tuneful world.
– *The Book of Invasions*, Vol. 2

# Contents

*The Book of Invasions – Lebor Gabála Érenn* (literally 'The Book of the Taking of Ireland') – is a compilation of eleven manuscripts describing the discovery of Ireland following the Creation and the Flood. Echoing the biblical account of the arrival of the Israelites to their Promised Land, the book records the first discoverer as a woman called alternatively Banba or Cessair – daughter of Noah's daughter Bith – who sailed off at her grandfather's suggestion to escape the coming Flood. She took with her a band of 150 women and three men in three ships. They were wrecked on arrival off the Irish coast and only fifty women survived (their names are given – Sella, Della, Duib, Addeos and so on) along with the three men, one of whom – Ladra – promptly died either from female excess or because an oar penetrated his buttock, while another – Fintan – escaped the women's demands by turning himself into a salmon.

Cessair's band lived in Ireland for forty years till destroyed by disease. They were followed two hundred years later by three Spanish fishermen whose boats were driven west by storm: Capa, Caigne and Luasat – 'a wright, a leech and a ruthless fisherman'. They returned to Spain and brought their wives back with them to settle. The book goes on to record other later arrivals, like Partholón who crossed the sea in his canoe, cleared the plains of their great woods and made 'the first building' and, as importantly, 'the first brewing'.

The text was intended for teaching and between the accounts are short snatches of verse that refer to the same events. They're usually incomplete – just the first few lines – and are presumed to be from well-known songs that would act as prompts to help students remember the story.

The book is written on vellum by several hands, notably by a scribe called Muirges mac Paidin who grumbles in the margins that the light he is working in is bad or that he has lost the piece of pumice he uses to smooth the vellum or that the ruler he has been given to line the page is too thick. He died, probably of irritation, in 1543.

It's a wayward, eccentric, fanciful history. The thing I like best about it is that in the vast record of time it ignores years and months quite routinely, while being very particular about day or hour. Cessair's ships for example came to land 'on the fifteenth, on a Saturday'.

1

We are living in another era of invasions. The newspapers are full of accounts of the movement of peoples: the English middle classes to the Mediterranean, Polish labourers to Cork, Kosovan women to Soho, Chinese property developers to Auckland, Iraqi doctors to London. Nudged by military takeovers or economic policies, by natural forces or by the decisions of bureaucrats in Washington or London, Geneva or Wellington, waves of invasion both violent and peaceable are set in motion.

When I heard about the Promised Land as a child, that paradise of milk and honey, I always imagined an empty land with honey bees nobody owned flitting over wide empty acres where the newcomers could let their cattle wander freely. It wasn't until years later that I realised the Promised Land had been densely inhabited and fiercely defended. I'd somehow missed that detail in Sunday school.

I am living in Ireland now for six months, looking out each day at a land my family left to emigrate to an archipelago in the southern Pacific. (On a Friday, no doubt. At 2 o'clock.) Invading, as they themselves had been invaded.

It is a strange feeling. These poems are about being here.

*Coolmona*
*Donoughmore, Cork*
*2006*

# The invasion

A hundred and fifty we were,
who set sail. Young and
clear-skinned, driven to the
edge of a bony country.

Some sat amidships
where the ride was easy.
Others bent to their paddling.
And three men amongst us.

So there we were on our good
ships, with their striped sails.
We crossed water to a long cloud
where we wrecked on a reef.

Fifty we were who came ashore.
Soaked from the sea and with
stonebruised feet. We lay down
in dry grass, and shared the men
around.

Till all of us had babies wriggling
up the dark stream, leaping all
obstacles.

We milked the men dry. One
died, another lived, and the
third became a salmon. He
turned cold in my arms and
silver-skinned. His eyes were
round and glassy. He flipped
from me to the stream and
got away. So I was left in
the long grass.

Slick drying on my belly,
the tiny fish swimming

## The Way of the Dishes

Today I followed the
Way of the Dishes.
From Kinvara to Keelhilla
along the greasy road.

The dishes flew before me.
Cups, plates and bottles of
red wine, a joint of beef,
stewed leeks and white
bread, sliced for eating.

I could see them floating
just ahead, set upon a white
cloth. I could see the flap of
it, rising to cross a hedge
like a flat fish swimming
through clear water and
me beneath like a small
sprat following.

To follow was not easy. The
dishes rode across country,
taking hedges and ditches on
their white wings, while I was
trapped by my car and the
narrow ways of men. I had
to turn corners and guess at
my final destination.

I saw the dishes fly to a
cliff face and drop behind
bare branches, hazel and ash.

I parked the car and found the
cloth come to ground,
embroidered hem fluttering
by the saint's bed. A heap
of fallen stone.

4

The saint was a lean man.
He picked at the beef and
poured salt over the leeks,
lest he be tempted.
He tossed his bread to the
sparrows and foreswore
the red wine, preferring
water from his blessed spring.

But his servant gnawed the bones
bare and spread good butter on his
bread. He drank his wine, thanking
whatever power it was that had
sent cloth and dishes, whatever
white hand it was that cooked
this food, and the kindly air that
carried it.

I watched from behind a tree as he
feasted while his master picked and
prayed. I watched his belly swell. I
heard him groan as his starved guts
cramped.

Within the hour he will be dead and
buried under a heap of stone.
While the saint will live,
revered by all for his restraint.

And the feast will grow mould,
the white cloth will rot and the
wine will turn to vinegar in
a tarnished cup.

## Spades

I have come to the land of
a thousand spades. And that's
only the one-sided spade.

Think another thousand with
two sides where a man might
press down with either foot.

Blunt-cornered or curved,
short-handled or long,
whole dialects of digging.

Men walked the roads here
carrying their chosen spade.
The fields were too small
for ploughs. Just room for
one man and the breadth
of his spade.

I think of my father and his
three spades: the one with the
square handle, smooth from his
hand. The long-handled shovel.
The narrow spade that was the
one preferred to dig the long
shaw.

And me allowed to follow
in his muddy track, carrying
the bucket and setting each
potato in black Kakanui loam
as he had shown me,

with its green shoot facing the sky.

## The Book of the Dun Cow

This is the book of the dun cow.
It is to be treated with reverence.
Stowed bound in silk, in silver.

The book is revered for the skin
from which its pages are made.
Skin of the dun cow.

Blessed cow of the saint. His
heifer with her twisted horn,
milk spilling from her swaying udder.

He loved her, followed her
wandering. Slept pressed to her side
on frosty upland. Her spindly calf.

And when she died cradled in straw
he skinned her, blade tugging at tufts
of belly hair, slitting neck and knee.

He stretched her skin, pegged it to
dry, legs splayed. Soaked it in his own
piss to soften, then cut it in squares,
shaven and stitched to make a book.

Now he is seated in a stone cell
to write the words that matter most
to him, on the skin of his dun cow.

But when his eyes tire with writing
he can rest his forehead on the desk
and smell it:

the scent of the dun cow and the
winding way she led him, the
damp lick of buttercups, the
green plop where he could
warm bruised feet, when the
way was all stones and frost
made the ground

too hard.

## The winner

The poet always wins
or the blind singer.

Butcher's shambles in
dust by the city wall or
spilled on office floor,
deals wrought behind
veneer while bullets
pierce the bronze wings
of angels. One two three.

Small arguments at
kitchen tables, doors
slamming on never.
Small hatreds small
betrayals small deaths
in smoke and falling
stone. Days that fade
to shouting.

No sign of victory in
the guts. A bloody mess.

Then the poet comes and
sees in the flop of failure
the outlines of some old
hero whom another poet
made from grunt and stab
on some muddy hill. And
there's that girl again, in
her buttoned coat, waiting
at the prison gate till her
husband dies.

She is listening for the
sound of bullets piercing
cotton shirt and snuggling
into lung and heart.

One two three.

And that's how
the song
will start.

## Blow-in

That bird has a name.
But I don't know it.
It may have three names:
Latin, English and Irish.
But I know none of them.

That wall, that road,
that hill, that precise
arrangement of stones
all have names. But I
don't know them.

That game, that song,
that man on TV, that
face on the magazine,
that town we passed
on the road in the dark.

That tree, that kind of
boat, that shop, that
street, that local hero,
that precise arrangement
of cloud.

They all have names.

But I can say only
road
hill
tree
cloud.

My great-grandparents
could not write. A shaky
cross marked receipt for
birth or death.

I can write, but in their
country I speak like a
bird whose tongue has
been split. Cut off at
its root. I perch on a
tree I cannot name and
chirrup:

road
hill
cloud
with my split tongue.

A straggler here.

A straggler there.

Blown in by
mighty winds.

## The little girl

My daughter looked for her
always. 'Where's the little
girl?' In pictures where
there was no child, she'd
look for her in rabbits,
cats or mice. The little
girl. Herself. 'That's me,'
she'd say, holding her
down with one finger.
'Now I'm in the story.'

And still I'm looking for
her: the little girl. In
history book or traveller's
guide, in footnote and news
report and the long record
of battle, law and poetry,
I look for her. The little girl.
The woman. The one who
looks like me.

The rabbit.

The cat.

The dancing mouse,
setting off on her adventures.

## Following cows

The road ends in a muddy yard.
Cows with their calves tear at
hay. We stand confused in
muddy boots. Lost our way.

The map shows a solid road.
Turn left, then right. The curve
of the hill harnessed to contour
lines. The end of a short day,
a single star, fading light.

The cows breathe deeply. Stretch
their heavy necks and trumpet at
walls of fallen stone. The country's
theirs, taken long since.

The rivers are named for them:
Boyne and Borora for white
cow and red, lakes where
calves wait under water.

Saints followed in their path
trusting their direction.
Roads twist and wind, woven
like the borders of a book and
following the slow saunter of
cows to water, byre or upland field.

We stumble over puggy ground
in sodden boots till we find tarmac
and the way home. While the path
forms over our heads: spilled milk
from a full udder, between banks of stars.

## Echo

These streets were water once.
Ships came to anchor where
there are shoe shops now, and
sandwich bars.

And tonight, rain making silk
of stone, the boats are back.
Patrick Street and Grand
Parade are become canals,
the skinny alleys their
tributary drains and ditches.

How this wet world glistens,
how it splashes!

And here's a drunk set sail
across the rolling tide. Yaws
and goes about then tacks
toward Shandon.

While the god with one
eye calls from the Post
Office corner.

How the wet world listens,
how his cry flashes,
marking the hidden reef!

Echo!

Echo!

Echo!

# The canoe in the National Museum

'Boardlike, noble and strong was his canoe.'
– Partholón, *The Book of Invasions*, Vol. 3

Black boat from a brown bog.
The line of it like a new moon
sailing. Cut from a single log.

Such hero oaks have gone, cut to
sail against Spain. There's hazel
brush over the stones, ranks of
spindly spruce squeaking on the
hilltops.

So this is how you feel, my
friend, before the waka that
had sailed clear through the
walls of the museum to
beach among whale bones.
Its feathers drab, no wind
to make them fly, no wave
to lift, no island to nudge aside.

This is how you feel, seeing
the adze bite left by a man
careful of bare toes, sweat
making his shoulders slick.

This is how you see them,
setting sail, baskets at their
feet and a little dog barking,
smoke rising from the huts
they are leaving, the river
opening out to the sea. Their
heads visible above the thwart
of the new moon.

You think of yours as I think of
mine, setting sail in their black
canoe.

The people the people the people.

15

## Beckett

He is everywhere, his head like
a bittern, pin feathers raised
among bulrushes.

He's festival of the month. Next
time it'll be Joyce or Flann O'Brien.
One City, One Book. A municipal
promotion.

His face is big in this dim room
where ladders reach to the top
shelf and the air is silent but
smells of shaven skins and
the quill feathers of dead
geese and ink squeezed from
oak gall and all those words
flying.

And on the street the man who
looks like Beckett sleeps on
torn cardboard. He is silent in
his blue sleeping bag, as silent
as if he slept on a river bank
among flag lilies and sweet
rushes. The noonday crowd is
brisk. It steps around him or
over him or around him,
while he lies still.

Waiting.

Waiting for . . .

No.

Just waiting.

## Lace

The girls are making crochet lace.
Barefoot, big toes splayed on
muddy stone, cracked skin stone
bruised, the blisters burst at night
with a scalding needle.

They stand with busy fingers,
serious for the camera. The
pattern lies in the twisting
thread. The hook dabs in
and out to find it and they
have no need to check. They
can make lace and talk or
watch the road, see the young
men pass by, their spades upon
their shoulders.

They face the camera squarely.
Don't pity us, they say. Or turn
us into postcards. And just to
make their point, they wear
their handiwork. White lace on
each dark dress. The web that
sets the face fair and underpins
their beauty.

## Cursing stones

My father was mannerly,
not given to swearing.

Perhaps among men, but
not in front of children.

When angered, he swore
in Irish.
Dom
in
um
deal.

Dom
in
um
deal
and slammed the door.

We did not know the words.
We heard only the syllables
of anger.

But now I know what he was
saying. In the only Irish left to
him he sent souls to the devil.

't'Anam 'on diabhal.'

The soul of Holyoake and
Lyndon Johnson the soul
of the car that would not
start the soul of the wife he
could not love the soul of
the work he could not stand
the soul of the war he could
not forget the soul of the
country he had left behind
the soul of the country he

had found the soul of the
evening paper the soul of the
wounded hand the soul of the
quarter-acre section the soul
of the roof that would not
stop leaking the soul of the
walls that would not stop
rotting. Turning the stones
and turning the stones
and turning the stones, sending
it all to that little grinding devil.

## Potatoes

I come from potato country.
The Potato Capital of New
Zealand. Gourmet King
Edwards laid out in boxes,
white stones set in gold.

King Edwards.
Ilam Hardy.
Cliffs Kidney.

They grow well, on sweet
soil. Limestone country,
thick loam on white bones.

My father planted his
quarter acre, dug the
ground in ridges, the
habit of farmers in a
boggy country, raising
their seed above rot.

Ridges like mountain ranges,
valleys between. Then the
leaves broke through and
we could crawl the length
of the green tunnels. Hidden
in the garden till the count
of ten when someone came
with a flaming sword and set
the roof on fire and we were
hunted out,

ready or not.

## Politics and economics

*Abbeystrewery, Skibbereen*


It's all politics, isn't
it? This patch of rough
ground where 9000
lie buried like spuds.
That's politics.

And this: the act of
writing. A hundred
years ago, these
fingers held a sacking
needle. My lungs
choked on jute.
Dead at 50. And a
needle in my hand,
not this sharp pen.

That's economics.

## Tarmac

They come ashore
scrambling like rats
for cover in the
tunnels under the
motorway, or
among coastal scrub.

Or crated, stacked
for dispatch, their
white bones visible
to the camera
through the walls
of a truck.

They all look the
same. Like that man
who is spreading
tarmac on the road.
Hooded, his eyes
averted, his bones
visible only to the
camera. Irish navvy
digging his canal,
Jewish ragman
wheeling his barrow,
Chinese miner
shouldering his shovel,
Russian whore
painting her wet mouth.

And those Italian
organ grinders
who turned the
handle to play
the same tune
over and over
while the monkey
danced on the
tarmac the
Sicilians had
newly laid
in Holborn.

## The Butter Road

We live near the Butter Road.
A straight line, leading direct
along a ridge to the city.

Once the wagons passed each
day and took the farmers'
cream, set yellow as buttercups
from the little jigging carts.

Sometimes we lose our way
on the drive home, confused
in twisting lanes laid down
by cows finding the kindest
contour.

Then we come upon this
straight line on its high ridge.

And know we're safe:
we have been rescued
by the Butter Road.

## Line

To begin with, the monolith
unadorned. A dancer, they said,
struck to stone by the saint.

Then lines and circles, like
leaf from a woven basket,
or the halo round the moon
on a foggy night or the
ripples left by a pebble
dropped into a spring.

Then the line becomes hard
to follow. Over and under
to a fox's head a dragon's
mouth an angel bull or eagle,
up and round the margins of
the page like brambles
round the small man who
sits bearing his heavy halo.

And his toes turned out
as if he planned to leap up
any minute now, jump the
line and begin

to dance.

## The News

What's the news?
What's the news?

Two old women cast
from their home by
former lingerie model,
her eyes laced tight as
a whore's corset.
Cleric lays finger on
open-mouthed altar boy.
Pink man in long black
coat avoids paying
millions in back tax.

What's the news?
What's the news?

Lithuanians die in minivan.
Polish workers underpaid.
Nigerians shot in drug war.
Carnage on roads.
Drive-by shooting.
Party ends in tragedy.
Bono for Pope.
Luxury hotel
for clifftop site.
A&E wards in crisis.

What's the news,
What's the news,
O my bold chevalier?
Of men marching north,
or electing not to march?

What's the news?
With your long-barrelled gun
your pike upon your shoulder
your songs and stones
your mortgages
and mobile phones
your site notice
celebrity lineup
your pint your parting glass.

What's the news?

My news is that we've switched
off the heaters, gone out bare armed
to see the cow in the next field
who has her own white calf.

Winter is past.

This is my news.

# The Speckled Book

'Four things are required by every work of
art: a Place, and a Time, an Author, and a
Cause of Invention.' – *The Speckled Book*

A book is like an
egg. It requires a
Place: a dark nest
of dry grass its
bardic bed.

And a Time. For
egg and book,
that's early
morning, early
spring. The time
for getting cracking.

The Author is
always to be found
curled in the shell,
like the dab of blood
that grows feathers
and becomes the
tuneful bird.

And the Cause of Invention
is the tune that is whistled
as the author pecks and pecks
within that speckled shell.

# Gobnait

She stands upon her beehive,
her cherubim at her feet
in their striped bodices.

Patron of bees. A jar of
honey by her well and a
baby's bib, necklaces and
earrings, car keys and
rosaries, a Darth Vader
doll in its black mask. A
striped cup hung from the
tree to sip her blessing.

Her church has no roof but
the sky. And by the open
window, the stone woman,
legs spread wide and her
crack rubbed smooth as
Peter's toe. Cows sing
their canticles from the
muddy yard beyond the
wall. Their udders sway
swollen with spring milk.

And bees fly among the
gravestones, bearing their
gospel of

busy and sweet.

# Genealogy

'a ready-made nucleus of degradation and disorder' (Carlyle)
'a tribe of squalid apes' (Froude)
– Two historians describe Irish immigrants to Scotland.


Vermin begat Squalor
who married the fourth son of
Hunger who fathered the Pig-
child and the Rat-daughter who
mothered Filth who bore
Raggy Mary who wed an
Empty Glass who was the
son of Not-enough-land whose
wife was Dull Superstition
daughter of Scratching
and Good-with-his-fists
who was descended directly
from Destitution who walked
the road in the company of
his limping sister Typhus
the White Skinned who
bore ten children to Feckless
the singing man who was
the son not of Man but of
Ape and danced to prove it
and the tenth child was Slum
Alley and the fourth was
Factory Fodder and the
seventh son of the seventh
son met his death in battle
before the walls of Profit,
but not before he had fathered
a child by Legs-Spread beneath
a bush on the Curragh. And
that soldier was Pat-the-Brute
and his child was Degradation
of the Crimson Hand who
lived to beget Disorder.

Sing of the race.
Sing of the line.

They may have other names
but these have not been
recorded by the historians.

## Sheela-na-gig

Here's the old one: the dark
hag with her slack breasts
and rattling ribs.

Splayed wide on castle wall
or over the church door,
drawing open the flaps of her
body like two curtains.

This is where you come from,
she says. This is where you
go. The cave. The cavern.
The crack.

She straddles the world
above the pit where we
hide among potatoes,
her cloak spread so that
we look up and say life,
life, and also, death.

She waits for us on either
side as if we lived in a
single room. All of us
crammed in, with her
outside the window in
the dark, or at the door.

The hag.

The great woman of the night
whom the tricky boy thought
to fool, till she said, 'That's
enough of that, my lad!' And
slammed her thighs
shut.

# The dogs of Ireland

The dogs of Ireland
lie in wait
at every driveway
every gate.

When we pass
they bark. It
is expected. Why
they're kept
and fed.

Then come along.
They lope ahead

Tails waving like
pennants,
toenails jigging
on tarmac,
balls bobbing.

Casual, so.
Rag tag psychopomp.

Just seeing where
the road might go.

## Betting

You cannot choose your
ancestors: say they are
three men, blown ashore,
a wright, a leech, and
a furious fisherman.

The wright: a capable
man with broad hands,
the kind who builds
boats but hugs the
coast. Who hammers
his wife and saws his
kids in two.

The leech: a feeble
hanger-on. A comedian
good for a laugh, but
never there when it's
his turn to pull in the net.
No hero.

And the one who takes
all the fish in the sea,
tears down all the trees,
makes a wasteland
where he breathes.

The founding fathers.

And you are their descendant
among their other thousands
of descendants, and you are
at the Mallow races, placing
a bet on the 2.05. A fiver
each way.

And there's the wright
checking the form and
making his cautious choices.

And the leech risking it all
– home, health and heart –
on a win.

And the furious fisherman
with his nets and quotas

who owns
all the horses.

## Gold

How they must have glistened,
the old ones. She in her moon
collar and golden rings. He in
his torque of twisted gold,
precious relic of the horsehair
rope and the man gasping,
going down for the good of
all. Pinned to the breast
of some stern goddess with
a precise arrangement of
hazelrods.

How they must have shone,
barefoot on stone, their ear
lobes pierced to hold these
golden boxes with their rattle
of golden peas.

The glitter of them with their
matted hair, on their shaggy
ponies riding the green miles
in that strange place that
reached all the way from

here

to there.

# Rolling over

I was born on a boat
that was rolling over.

Wrecked on a reef it
was rolling from east
to west and the bones
of it were being
lifted up. White stone.

White stone and tarry
soil: Kakanui silt,
Taiko loam.
The richest soils
in New Zealand.
The purest stone.

My bones are made of
white stone. The stone
is made of white bone.
A universe of tiny
beings born in shells
like hinged boxes.

They breathed and fed
and rotted, died three
times in their shells
and were restored.

This is the life cycle
of the bryozoa.

I was made of stone
born on the wreck,
of a black canoe
on an island
in an archipelago
in Oamaru
North Otago
Otago

South Island
New Zealand
The World
The Solar System
The Universe

Set like a white spud
in tarry soil as the
ground beneath our feet
was rolling over.

## Ballad

There is the song that is sung
at the leaving. The farewell
from the quay. For the pride,
the rose, the bright star,
who are all sailing away.

*Hero with his cardboard*
*suitcase. Bard with his*
*guitar. And Beauty in her*
*new shoes . . .*

Waving from the rail as
they set sail on the third,
led by a leaping salmon
and a cunning little bird.

But before their ship has
sailed far, the tune begins
to fade, to sentimental
humming and la la la . . .

And before the ship has sailed far,
the Hero's turned to sin and the
Bard's a drunken scoundrel
and Beauty's shed her skin.

*Hero with his cardboard*
*suitcase. Bard with his guitar.*
*And Beauty in her new shoes . . .*

And when the ship comes close to
land, they smash upon the reef:
not Hero, Bard and Beauty,
but Oppressor, Judge and Thief.

And the suitcase cracks wide open
to release its glittering swarm
of beads and seeds and cloth
too thin to keep a body warm.

And the Bard slumps in a doorway
singing something vague
while Beauty's shoes leave
gaping holes where e'er she walks,
and their soles unleash a plague.

And the land that they have come to
to escape the coming flood is stripped
to rock and tarmac and sour red mud.
And its cost is arms and legs and minds
and sour red blood.

And the land that they were promised
when they fled from hollow hunger
was the milky land, the honeyed land
that they dreamed when they were
green and younger.

When Hero, Bard and Beauty
set sail on the third
led by the leaping salmon
and the cunning little bird.

And their bold ship sailed

across

and across

and across

the lines between
what everybody knows.

To where the salmon
drifts in a murky sea
and the bird sings alone
in her silent tree:

'So it goes.

(La la.)

So it goes.'

*Hero with his cardboard suitcase.*
*Bard with his guitar.*
*And Beauty in her new shoes . . .*

## How I'd take the country

I'd arrive on a Saturday,
come in from the south
and hop from rock to
rock where the trees all
point north with bony
fingers.

I'd come dressed as a
bird to circle that place
in Abraham's Bosom
where the seven gills
swim upriver intent
upon breeding. Then
hang above the Lindis
where the hills stand
back watching, with
their brown arms
folded, saying summer.

Then shift shape to cow.
A cow on a truck, passing
through any small town
with its dead soldiers
at the crossroads and
its pies in the warmer.

A fish would be best for
the reach of clinking
shingle where millions
beach, jittery as broken
glass and wriggling fast
for the cover of their
own deep creek.

As god I'd stride upon
the mountain that was
my black canoe, wrecked
upon the reef with its
brave prow smashed
and its hull scraped bare
and buzzing with sub
division.

The bush would best
be taken as a fly or
some small glittering
thing, nibbling and
sipping.

But for the city street,
be human. Walk about
among your people,
buying shoes or taking
notes or sitting at a table
on a footpath, recalling

New York

or Babylon.

## Midden

Words are piled deep
here. Middens of
language, dungheaps
of song, a slurry of
history spread thick
on every field.

The battle, the king,
the insult, the lament,
the lovemaking, the
betrayal, the debate,
the refusal, the birth,
the vision, the law
making, the source,
the coming ashore,
the leave taking.
Site of ambush,
site of treaty, site
of the former home,
site of the movie,
site of the shipwreck,
site of the book,
site of the poem
that was translated
from the song
sung by the traveller
woman and a poet
set upon his plinth
at the end of every
main street. Poet
and Patriot.

With every inch
spoken for where
can you begin to
dig with your shiny
new spade?

Where set out the
seed you've saved?

And how long till
you break through
to solid stone?

## Waving

They wave on the roads
round Donoughmore:
a quick flick of the hand
as they drive past, or off
the wheel completely.

Hullo! they say and
Hiya! Howyadoin?

So it is to be expected
that their saint would
wave too. Here's his
skinny arm raised
in its glass case
at the National
Museum. Of bronze,
finely wrought, with
silver fingernails.

The hand within, the
fragments of bone,
his arm no bigger
than a child's. The
skin tattooed with
prayer, plain bone
pulsing through
metal, making

all things well.

The saint waves from
his cabinet among the
other curiosities.

The cursing stones.
the daggers, the stone
goddess facing in all
her three directions:

The holy trinity of

Hullo!

And Hiya!

And the third for

Howyadoin?

## Well

The lad in the Formula One cap
points the way across a field.
Spring grass green tongues
licking pocked soil kicked up
by wintering cows. His dog,
a loping spaniel, comes along.

And there she stands in the
far corner, both arms raised in
greeting by her spring. Palms
facing forward, fingers spread.
Her bare body plump, with
heavy thighs, and a cross
scratched on breast and belly,
quartering her as if she were
fresh bread, a white loaf
newly risen.

Bubbles break around her,
burst from shingle and make
circles of the water, rings that
flash and vanish.

There's a seat for breathing.

New leaf for asking.

Bubbles for listening.

Spread hands for giving.

Striped cup for taking.

And a spaniel for just
sniffing about, splashing
in a holy spring and being
happy, right this minute.

## The Lonely Planet visits the dead

So much time spent visiting the
dead: the sites of battle and of
ambush. Stone soldiers on every
corner with column and wreath.

Remember death. The massacre
at dawn, the final words, the last
supper, the methods of execution.

Why not a memorial to the kids
who played between the wars?
Made goalposts of the memorial,
and a play house of the scaffold.
Who took the stones for hopping,
the burnt fuselage for pedal cars,
and the hangman's rope for
skipping.

Don't miss the sight of the girls
in the main square, where they
leap up and over, chanting
anthems composed from the
initials of all the boys they plan
to love.

# Rail

He saw it once: Ireland.
A smudge from the ship's
rail as they sailed out
from the Clyde.

'Come here!' his mother
said. Cheeks flushed,
breath short, jute dust
from the sacking factory
making old rope of her
lungs.

She lined them up at the
rail: all her children. One
two three four five six.

'That's Ireland,' she said.

Their distant home away
from wherever they might
be. They gazed from the
rail like gangly calves at
those distant greener fields.

## Crop

*Flourball*
*May Queen*
*Land Leaguer*
*Ulster Chieftain*

Let us recite
the tribe
of Lumper.

12 pounds per man,
10 pounds per woman
per day. With milk
and butter the perfect
food, making men
jump and giving
the girls of Ireland
their fair complexion.

*Kerrs Pink*
*Golden Wonder*
*Epicure*
*Snowflake*

The people sit
upon their walls
lamenting the loss
of all their crops.

*Fir Apple*
*Thome Black*
*Irish Queen*
*Ash Leaf Kidney*

The typical beggar
is a ragged woman
with five or six
children at foot.

*Main Crop*
*Peru Purple*
*Gladstone*
*Shamrock*

Thin men make
walls for thin soup
break rock
not bread
for roads that lead
in a straight line
to nowhere.

*King Edward*
*Champion*
*Cliffs Kidney*
*Arran Banner*

There's no eating
to them, shrunk
to the skin. Just
the bare bones
of the feast.

On the last day
they swell. They
seem plump and
well. Then the
belly splits. They
burst. Then they
are tossed out.

Children of
the tribe of
Lumper

with their
fine bruised
skins.

## Lissadell

Fog on Benbulben's broad back
like the breath of a brown bull
taking his ease in a green field.

Fog on Knocknarea where the
stones swell round Maeve
who dreamed and fought for
a brown bull. Buried standing
upright, her white bones
clasped about the memory
of a sword.

Welcome to Yeats Country!
Visit the Yeats Tavern!
The Yeats Café!
See where the poet has
spread his dreams
under your feet!

See the lake isle floating
on its dream of green beans!

See the stones of Lissadell
swollen round the dream of
those two girls floating through
empty rooms like fog.

Before silk was swapped
for army serge and daisies
for a gun.

Before that long evening
when light hangs like
a curtain between night
and day.

The greasy chair.
The tepid cup.

And all the heroes
gone to play for
Man. United.

## Hunting

Father Lynch remembers
hunting with the Aghabullogue
and his curate, Father
Casey, who knew no
fear.

Putting their faith in
God and a pair of big bay
hunters, they cleared bank
and stone wall, riding hard
behind the baying pack.

But the Bishop disapproved.
Said No More and the priests
of Donoughmore gave up
their horses and the leaping
of walls.

For a life of small
repeated gestures.

Christening and
first communion.

The wedding and
the funeral tea.

And the

drip

drip

drip

of small omissions.

But at its end, a memory of
ice cracking on muddy
puddles like the eucharist,
and a big bay hunter sweating
between his thighs and
charging fences like the
Son of Man, and the fox,
tangled in briars, torn to pieces
by the baying pack, and the
smear of its blood that is
dabbed on the foreheads

of all true believers.

## The Battler

This is the book they call
The Battler. The one held
high before the army as
they marched to battle.
Led by the songs of the
dancing king, the shepherd
leading his flock to their
green pastures.

Words form legions and
stride in the first rank,
armed to the teeth with
syllables.

Men follow, chanting
the synopsis.

The book is truth the
word of god or desert
patriarch, the book is
the life of the saint or
the housepainter or
turn the page and here
is Mr Missile with
his gobby grin who
is just three frames
away from destruction.

And the word is
burn baby burn
burn baby burn
burn baby burn

as new men pursue
The Battler and the
words that scurry
into the scrub of
a desert scraped

flat as a blank page.

## Poet, Novelist and above all Patriot

The poets have taken over
the city. They have sealed
the harbour and occupied
the square.

The novelists have their
emplacement on the high
tower. Playwrights patrol
the walls. And all the
people have gone out to
fight armed with their
phrases.

That publican is not to be
trusted. He is breaking the
code of glasses. That road
gang spilling tar has a
map of songs concealed
in their mucky truck.

And over on the tangled
bank where the ranks
are drawn up to face
the usual compromise,
the women shriek like
hoodie crows. They
flap between the lines,
calling on ordinary people

to rise up and act like
the heroes they
have heard about

in stories.

## The brown bull

We left on a green day
from a green mountain.
Five we were, and a
brown bull. Calves
at foot.

Penned on the deck of
a shaky craft we sailed.
Damp straw our bedding
grey hay our feeding
red water our drinking
and the brown bull
swept over, running
and running away up
the sheer slope of a
green mountain.

This is where we came
ashore. They paused to
stare at four legs, horns,
and shrunken udders.

They stared: the natives
with their two legs,
two wings.

Their trees fell before
us. We took the land
with our steady tread.

The earth puckered.

And the brown bull
grazing, among flecks
of white foam,

like daisies,

like mountain
flowers.

## Seed

The seed hooks on to
fleece or blows in across
water. Sets root on
shifting soil, like this bog
that lies like a blanket
over a restless sleeper.
One dark deep eye
opens. Another closes.

So was I carried in a
man's wrinkled pocket,
caught in the seam like
fluff. So was I borne as
a bead in a woman's
bag, waiting my turn
to drop and roll in the
dark.

So were we carried in.
Concealed. Unobserved.
Small things that took
root in wet places

reaching down to solid
earth through the cracks
in broken tarmac.

## The flood

Spring has swept
in, every hedge
crested white.

We walk between
breakers as if this
were the way to the
promised land and
Pharaoh and his
chariots rattling
after.

To the lake where
the dam has made
black broken work
of oak and ash.

The wave broke
over the Gearagh,
drowned its names
and houses, lanes
and fields. Water
at the step where
the dog sat
scatching sunlight
water at the step
where the women
sat chatting birdsong
water at the step
where the man
stamped home
in muddy boots.

The lake ripples
over harrowed land.
Light and heat its
glittering harvest.

I remember that
dry valley, briar
and mingimingi
and the flags raised
high on a brown
hill to show where
the water would
reach.

And us standing
looking up at the
sky as if we were
already drowned.

At our feet a heap
of cracked bone.

And at our backs
the bus waiting
to carry us all

to the place of
the star.

# Road

They dug deep with sharpened
shovels. Good spadesmen all.
Dug wide. Built a road where
each stone bears a bony name.

O'Connell and Mulligan,
Slaven, Lynch and Connor,
Healey and O'Toole.

Each stone stacked like a skull
in a broken arch. The road they
made is broad and flat enough
for bare feet. The view from
the top is over a field wrinkled
with old crops. By the wall a
space called Broadway where
people slept under branches
like those small birds that
have no names. Or in tents
of ox hide where the visions
ran like rain.

The road leads from the ditch
straight across the field into
a hill. As if a door might
open there. As if there might
be castles below ground,

with banquets and gardens

and birds like sapphires,

singing.

# The long way round

Last night I dreamed the long
way round. Followed the crater
rim from Hilltop to Cabstand.

The narrow road along the edge
where the bubble burst sharp
as a broken bottle.

Harbour on one hand with
its clenched and bloody fist.
Outer bays on the other,
tucked into the mist.

I crisscrossed the breaking
point between bare hills,
bare stone, cracked rib of
matai. Totara's pelvic bone.

Dodged round molten rock
where tussocks tossed
their tangled hair like
daughters laughing they
don't care, they don't care,
each fine strand gleaming.

Last night I dreamed the long
way round and it became my
own, by right of dreaming.

# Hair

She has the hair of queens and
warriors. The mane of Maeve
dyed red and gold, the mane of
Cúchulainn fighting at the ford.

Her hair is tangled like the twigs
of a hawthorn tree, woven so
tightly that, should she sleep
beneath an apple tree and should
an apple fall, it would catch in the
net of her hair.

She would not waken. She
might stir, dreaming of gravity
and the way the world is. That
sweet pippin of a planet fallen
from its dark tree. She would
catch the apple in her hair,
among shells and beads, carved
bone and the buttons from her
grandmother's button box.

Her hair wild as mingimingi
as she rides down on the legions
of grey order, shouting the
slogan of her people:

Myself Alone!

# The Hag of Beare

The woman in Ardgroom
is doing her accounts, her
wrinkled hand with its gold
rings filing receipts.

She points the way to the
Hag. Marks it on the map.

Squat rock in a rocky field.
Each wrinkle laced with
gold coin begging favours.

Old rock, blown in
molten from thin air.

Old woman from whose
apron these mountains
tumbled like fresh eggs.

She sits at her ease
surveying her creation.

Those houses sucked
pink and yellow by a
childish wind. The lads
in their tractors cutting
another crop. That small
boat going
smack
smack
smack
at every crinkle
on its way out.

I give her my pen.
Leave it in her lap
among the pennies.

## The Lament of the Nun of Beare

*a translation*

Ebb to me!

In old age, the tide turns,
brings back the blood
and I grieve at its coming,
yet am glad at the flood.

I am the nun of Beare.
Once my dresses were new.
Now my shift is so thin
my bones show through.

I loved people, not riches,
when I was alive.
Loved their wide plains
over which I could drive.

Swift chariots I had
and horses fleet.
Bless the kings who
gave them to me!
Now they hand me a
penny whenever we meet.

My body is fearful
of this Son of God
and the judgement
he'll make when I'm
under the sod.

Bony my hands now
that once touched
splendid men.
Too bony to rise over
sweet boys again!

Girls laugh and delight
at the coming of spring.
But I, an old woman,
have sorrows to sing.

No wedding lamb for my
table. I pour no good ale.
My hair grey and scanty
beneath a white veil.

Once I wore coloured
veils over my hair.
Now my veil is white,
and I no longer care.

Nothing old do I envy
but Femin's wide plains.
Storms rage – yet they
spring goldenhaired
once again.

Tonight in the darkness
the winter waves roar.
No king's son nor slave's
son will visit my door.

I am cold. Wear a shawl
to sit in the sun.
Winter slips in to smother.
Youth's summer is done.

I was wanton in youth
and I'm glad I was bold!
If I'd been more cautious
I'd still sit here: old

in my ancient cloak –
when the bare hills' covering
is the fine icy cloak
flung down by the King.

God help me! Whose bright eyes
to candle feast were the spark,
now dim in a wooden church,
decayed in the dark.

Mead and wine with kings
I drank in my day.
Now I sit with old women
drinking water and whey.

May I drink from this cup!
May my blood turn from rage!
May I accept as God's will
this chilly old age!

May I accept as my cloak
this grey hair that on me
grows through my skin as
lichen on a gnarled tree.

My right eye snatched from me
as payment and due.
To complete the transaction,
my left eye taken too.

Flood surge and swift ebb.
What is brought to your hand,
the ebb draws from you.
This, I understand:

Flood surge and swift ebb.

I know these to be so.

I have fed all from my pantry.
I have never said 'no'.

I have taken in strangers,
I have done my best.
Now the Son of Man
is my only guest.

Happy the island
in the midst of the sea,
for flood follows ebb.
But not for me.

Sad my dwelling and
empty, on this bare day.

I must learn from
my sadness:

that all ebbs away.

## Dance

To spin knowing
where the feet must
land to follow the
line that twists and
crosses other lines
like the tracks left
by cattle on a bare
hillside marking the
way to rock and
water or back to
warm straw to know
the pattern drummed
on a dusty floor as if
it were a bare page
where feet tap the
code of advance retreat
join hands form a star
turn within the circle
of a steady arm to
dance the mathematics
of eight then four
then two then one.

To know the land and
its warm rock twisted
by aeons of advance
retreat the code of
cattle the circles of
stone marking the
mathematics of stars
the steady drum of
bare feet the cross
on the hillside the
dusty page where
numbers dance one
then two then four
then eight in the

pattern that leads
all dancers beneath
the hillside where
water spins its lines
between fields
of golden straw.

## Bed

Ends fray tangle split / and tug
bowels choke veins plug / alone
on that dark bardic / bed all
men are seers all / women
shifted shape to bird / or cat
and memory sits / chill on
the tongue like a pen / ny sucked
as a baby sucks / its spoon.

In that dark room the / faces
rise like many moons / gleaming,
like moons at harvest / shining
on fields of slaughtered / stubble.

This is the classic / structure:
seven syllables / for life
enough for seven / stages
a caesura at / the fifth
where the line trips and / falters
and then the poem / starts to
run like a child on / its way
home wanting only / the kit
chen door, the dog wait / ing, the
worn step that is the word where
the poem starts and / where it

ends.

# The verb 'to be'

It *is* foggy.
There *is* a mountain.
I *am* climbing the mountain.
She *is* climbing the mountain.
The path *is* slippery.
She says, 'It *is* all right.
It *will* all *be* all right.'
She *is* right.
There *are* people behind us.
They *are* climbing the mountain.
They *are* in the fog.
Their voices *are* broken.
There *is* a shout.
There *is* laughter.
We *are* all climbing the mountain.
She *is* climbing ahead of me.
There *is* fog in her hair.
Her hair *is* glittering.
The wind *is* cold.
There *is* a man with a walking stick.
There *are* names scratched on
the stick.
He carries the names as if
they *were* eggs.
They *could* fall and smash.
We *are* carrying names too.
They *are* carved on bone.
They *are* scratched on skin.
We *are* all carrying names
up the mountain.
There *is* a chapel at the top.
It *is* locked.
Its walls *are* damp.
There *is* broken timber.
There *are* fallen stones.
It *is* cold here.
Now we *are* turning.
We *are* going down.
She *is* running.

She *is* sliding down the mountain.
I *am* following her.
She *is* running ahead in the fog.
That *is* how it *is* now.
That *is* how it *will be*.
That *is* how it *will be*
till she *is* and I *am* not.
She *will be*.
I *will* not *be*.

The verbs slip under our boots,
like small changeable stones.

## Daffodils

No words to start. No
names. Trees learned
the land by touching
it with dumb fingers.

The names flew in
and hovered, light
as mayflies, skimming
the river of the white
calf, the hill of gorse,
the crag of the cat.

They shifted shape,
became other things.
The river is black
now and deep, the
hill is the hill of
hanging, and the
cats have been
butted from the
crags by shaggy
saints.

As my house
stands on the lip
of the bailer of a
black canoe.

And on a heap
of broken timber.

And on a green shoot.

And on the rocky
point of a man.

Or named Long Bay,
plain words,
printed out
in daffodils.

But already, look:
they've multiplied.

Gone wild.

Danced over the lines.
Invaded the field.

They are popping up
in odd places, as if they
have forgotten completely

how to spell.

## Marginalia

Poems should stand by themselves – and I hope these do – but when I go to readings I like the asides, just as I like the footnotes in books and the marginal scribblings of an irritable scribe.

*The invasion, p. 3.* 'Who was the first to take Ireland after the creation of the world? This is what the Book of Druim Snechta says, that Banba was the name of the first woman who found Ireland before the Flood and that from her Ireland is called "Banba". With thrice fifty maidens she came and with three men. Forty years were they in the island: thereafter a disease came upon them so that they all died in one week. Afterward Ireland was for 200 years without a living person . . .

> It is there that they came to harbour
> the woman-crowd at Dun namBarc
> in the Nook of Cessair, in the lands of Carn
> on the fifteenth, on a Saturday.'
> – *The Book of Invasions*, Vol. 2

*The Way of the Dishes, p. 4.* The Burren is a landscape in western Ireland composed of striated limestone, stripped by glaciers to form smoothly contoured hills, bare and grey white – pavlova hills – or expanses of flat stone pavement, cracked in orderly rectangles like huge tiles. I visited it over four days in late winter when the bare bones of the place were particularly compelling. The topographical map marked 'St Mac Duach's Bed', the 'Servant's Grave' and something called 'The Way of the Dishes'.
    I drove along little twisting roads through fog to a gate at the foot of a hill. There were no signs or maps or general interpretative fiddle faddle, just a faint track across the flags that looked like the marks left by the narrow wheels of small carts. There were cattle in the fields but the ground was not pocked by their hooves: the land looks too bare and rocky for farming but the sharp drainage makes it ideal for cattle, especially over winter, and the grass that grows between the pavements is especially rich in nutrients so they fatten well. Between the stones in the deep regular cracks, called 'scailps' or 'grykes', grow a great variety of plants (600 species have been recorded – the greatest concentration in Ireland) in a unique mix of tundra and Mediterranean varieties. Gentians grow here at sea level alongside orchids and maidenhair fern. I followed the grooves in the limestone to the piles of stone that were the grave of the servant and the saint's bed at the foot of a cliff: bare branches, wet rock and that stillness you get when the fog is down.

The legend is as it is told in the poem: of a feast that flew from King Guaire's castle to feed the saint at Easter. On the way home I passed the monastery the king built for the saint near Gort: a ruined complex of church, chapels, living quarters and a high tower, needle-sharp amid a cluster of gravestones with their loving arrangements of brilliantly coloured plastic carnations and ribbons.

*Spades, p. 6.* Near where I have been living at Donoughmore is the Blarney River valley where for over a hundred years the Monard and Coolowen Ironworks produced the thousands of varieties of shovels and spades required by the Irish market. I like tools: when my parents died, I kept my mother's washboard and the white stick she used to draw out the clothes from the copper. And I kept a little hand hoe my father made from a piece of wood and some bent iron for scuffing up the weeds between the rows of vegetable seedlings.

*The Book of the Dun Cow, p. 7. The Book of the Dun Cow* is a compilation of prose and verse in Irish transcribed by monks at the great monastery of Clonmacnoise around AD 1100. It was widely believed that its vellum pages had been cut from the skin of a dun cow, Odhar, who accompanied the founder of the monastery, St Ciaran, when he left home to live the life of a monk. Odhar's milk sustained the monastery. The saint drew a line on the ground between her and her calf with his staff and thereafter the holy cow licked her calf over the line, but never let it suckle, so that she always had enough milk for her human charges.

After her death, Odhar's skin remained sacred. Cattle skins were highly regarded as agents of visions up until the eighteenth century in both Ireland and Scotland: there is record of a man who could not sleep because of the fleas in his bedding. He wrapped himself instead in an ox hide he found laid over a chair in his chamber and as a result stayed awake for three days and nights, experiencing visions.

The book, as a relic of the saint and his holy cow, was highly valued. It was, for example, handed over in 1380 as ransom for an O'Donnell prince who had been captured – along with some highly prized chairs – by enemies.

The text contains historical and religious material and the earliest known versions of several famous tales that date from the pre-Christian era, most notably the *Táin Bó Cúailgne*, the story of how Queen Maeve sent her army on one of the cattle raids that were the noble sport of their era to capture a precious brown bull from the herds owned by the men of Ulster. This story was supposed to have been written by the saint himself on vellum cut from Odhar's skin.

*The winner, p. 8.* What did I know before I came to Ireland in the winter of 2006? Very little – though my father called himself Irish and my first husband was a linguist who studied Old Irish. (I saw the moon landing while at a Celtic languages conference in Dublin in 1969.) I had read books by Irish writers, from Joyce to Marian Keyes. From Yeats I knew 'nine bean rows will I have there' (we had sung a version of that at school) and 'a terrible beauty is born' but nothing of what that beauty might have been, and who was Connolly? Or Pearse?

To travel to Ireland is to fill in the gaps between tags of song or verse. Drive to Dingle and you pass through Castlemaine, humming 'The Wild Colonial Boy'. Or to Tralee, and there is that pale moon rising. Or north, where the Mountains of Mourne are sweeping down to the sea . . .

The gaps around Yeats's terrible beauty began to be filled in when I visited Kilmainham Gaol in Easter Week, a sunny blowy day walking over the hilltop above the Liffey. Inside the gaol, the sun and all movement of air vanished, excluded by blocks of damp limestone. There was no signage, just a compelling story told by a guide who could tell a story well, beginning in the chapel where Joseph Plunkett married Grace Gifford on the night before his execution in 1916. A plain room, with an altar and rows of wooden benches. A corridor with its rows of cells each with a single printed name over the door. The stone-breaking yard where they were shot, Connolly tied to a chair for he was too weak from wounds to stand.

Easter 2006 marked the anniversary of their deaths with a military procession down O'Connell Street. To me it looked like all such parades, with too many trucks and not enough bands, and ranks of soldiers marching past the dear leader in his long black overcoat. I felt confused by it, just as I feel confused by the internecine killings and ambushes of the Civil War. And the fact that Ireland remained neutral in 1939–45, a time referred to here as 'The Emergency'. And that de Valera offered his condolences to the German ambassador on the death of Hitler.

The statue at the foot of O'Connell Street opposite the Post Office has four bronze seated angels with spread wings. The bronze is pierced with bullet holes from a time when right and wrong seemed more straightforward: the enemy has a gun boat on the Liffey and the rebels hold the Post Office. And the song has the last word.

*Blow-in, p. 10.* Any newcomer to this southwestern part of rural Ireland is a 'blow-in'.

*Following cows, p. 13.* The Irish word for road is *bóthar*, and means 'cow way'. Country roads wind along old trails, and were designed to accommodate the width of two cows. Cows have been fundamental to Irish life for millennia. Major rivers often have 'cow' as part of their name, suggesting their role in nourishing the land just as milk nourished the people. Before the Irish became potato eaters, their basic diet was milk and curds in summer, and butter – preserved in wooden barrels and kept fresh by being buried in bogs – in winter. (The barrels are still found occasionally by peat diggers: a friend tells me he tasted the butter from such a barrel and it was still edible.)

*Echo, p. 14.* On our first day in Cork I went to get a mobile phone. Cork city is centred on an island ('Corcaigh' means 'marshy') where the River Lee branches on meeting the sea. The largest street, Patrick Street, was a canal until the eighteenth century. It curves along the length of the island and narrow laneways veer from it at odd angles. It's confusing at first, especially on a wet afternoon, already getting dark though only 4 o'clock, and there was a strange repetitive echoing call from the corner opposite the Vodafone shop: it took me a while to work out that it was the newspaper man calling out the name of the evening paper, the *Echo*.

*Beckett, p. 16.* In summer 2006, Dublin was celebrating Samuel Beckett. At Trinity – where he had once been a student – there was an exhibition of his manuscripts, letters and assorted photographs. Downstairs: The Book of Kells and long queues in the gift shop. Upstairs: the barrel-vaulted Long Room with its cliff faces of leather-bound books, marble busts of eighteenth-century worthies, and the fly-away, flimsy display boards of the exhibition.

*Cursing stones, p. 18.* Such stones were kept in old churches or other hallowed places. A person who felt they had been wronged would perform some ritual of fasting and prayer, then turn the stones, or employ the person who knew the appropriate words to do so, to bring about retribution. On Inis Mor, sister island to Yeats's Innisfree on Lough Gill and site of a former bardic school, there is a collection of cursing stones. They are laid on a larger slightly concave rock like the fossilised eggs of some strange and massive bird.

*Politics and economics, p. 21.* The area round Cork suffered greatly during the Famine. In Donoughmore alone 1400 people died in the winter and spring of 1846–47, including the priest who ministered to the dying. It is common to see road signs reading 'Famine Graveyard' pointing off down some muddy lane to a patch of rough ground, walled away from grazing by cattle. At Skibbereen, one of the largest such graveyards lies beside a busy road on the riverbank.

Like over a million others, my ancestors fled the country mid-century, to find work in the jute factories of Dundee. On official documents recording births or marriages or deaths they signed their names with a cross.

*Tarmac, p. 22.* Ireland in 2006 is undergoing a dramatic transformation. Boosted by euro funds, building is booming. Every town and village sports its subdivision, pink and yellow executive residences spring up overnight in country fields, and coastal properties are changing hands for astronomical figures. Property magazines for the Irish investor appear alongside the girlie magazines at the newsagents. Every Sunday afternoon there are property fairs in hotel foyers, designed to attract the newly rich into buying holiday apartments in Bulgaria, Cyprus, anywhere with a reliable summer and a glimpse of a distant ocean . . .

The boom is fuelled by returnees: for the first time, young Irish people are coming home to employment rather than leaving in their millions for London or New York. Emigrants are also arriving en masse, particularly from Eastern Europe: the woman behind the coffee machine will be from Estonia, the builders on the house site across the road will be Polish, while in Gort near Lady Gregory's Coole Park where Yeats's wild swans 'paddled the cold companionable streams', the square fills each morning with crowds of stocky, dark-haired Brazilians. Brought over first to staff a meat-packing factory, the men now wait for the vans that take them to casual outdoor work while the women work as cleaners. They make up a third of the town's population. In Gort, a friend told us, 'getting a Brazilian' means a trim hedge and a shiny bathroom, and not Posh Spice's favourite brand of topiary.

Soon after we arrived in Donoughmore a tarmac gang began working on driveways along the road. The boss was a young Irishman who sat in his Merc chatting on the cellphone, and the gangers were Lithuanians – just as in the nineteenth century, the gangers who tarmacked London's streets were the newly arrived Sicilians.

*The Butter Road, p. 23.* Cork is dairy country. When we arrived we woke each morning to the whirr of milking machines long before daybreak. When we walk along the roads, we often have to wait for a long line of cows to pass over: big black and white Holsteins with heavy udders and uncertain bowels.

Butter was exported from Cork in great quantity throughout the nineteenth century, to supply domestic markets in Britain and elsewhere and especially to supply the British army, for it was heavily salted and stored in wooden firkins so it lasted well. The market was destroyed by the arrival of New Zealand butter that was chilled and therefore less salty and more palatable.

*Line, p. 24.* There are many traditions of stone circles being the remains of dancers – often women – who were turned to stone by some disapproving saint.

The saints in The Book of Kells with their enormous heavy haloes sometimes seem very small among all the curvilinear work. I like their curly hair and the way their ankle bones are drawn.

*The News, p. 25.* 'I have news for you' is the beginning of an early Irish seasonal poem.

'What's the news? What's the news?' is the beginning of 'Kelly the Boy from Killarne', a terrific swagger of a song about that classic Irish subject: military defeat. It was my father's favourite song, best sung after a few beers at the Second NZEF.

*The Speckled Book, p. 27.* The *Leabhar Breac* or 'Speckled Book' of MacEgan is a compilation of saints' lives and Irish history dating from the fourteenth century. It is also known as 'The Book of Battles' – but these old Irish books were often known by the colour of their bindings: the *Leabhar Buidhe* or 'Yellow Book', the *Leabhar Dubh* or 'Black Book'. The *Leabhar Breac* is held in the library of the Royal Irish Academy.

As for the whistling – my younger daughter works with endangered bird species and tells me that you know when an albatross egg is nearly ready to hatch because you can hear the chick whistling inside the shell.

*Gobnait, p. 28.* Gobnait is the name of a revered saint. Girls are given her name, and her holy well at Ballyvourney is much visited. Children are brought there in their white dresses and tiaras at the time of their first communion. I visited it just after her feast day which is on 11 February, a few days after Brigit's on 1 February. Both saints are thought to be descendants of the one goddess Brigit, who long before Christianity took her under its wing was a major Celtic divinity worshipped throughout Europe as patron of fire, metal working and writing, among other things.

Gobnait's well is up a side road among trees covered in thick green moss. It is surrounded by little offerings: bunches of daffodils in early spring, rosaries hung from the branches of trees just beginning to bud, dozens of little votive figurines and personal things like hair ties and children's toys and necklaces and baby's bibs. Her church and statue are round the corner next to a muddy cowyard. Her statue stands in an enclosure, and across the road is her church – not the towered building, which is Protestant and was built in the eighteenth century, but the roofless ruin beside – and the mound that is her grave, which pilgrims have circled for hundreds of years, sometimes barefoot, sometimes on their knees, repeating an exact sequence of prayer and invocation.

*Genealogy, p. 29.* There's a picture I like by Ford Madox Brown of workmen digging up Hampstead High Street. A group of navvies – two with spades, one red haired and noble, one swigging mightily from a tankard, one who seems to be singing with his head flung back and his mouth open – are at its centre, digging. One of the two gentlemen reclining on the railing observing their toil and lamenting the advent of machinery and the loss of honest creative labour, is Carlyle. When I look at it I am planning the next frame, the one where the red-haired navvy says, 'Oops' and dumps some muck on the historian's polished boots. But perhaps the housemaid who used the first manuscript of Carlyle's history of the French Revolution to kindle the fire one morning acted in his stead.

I don't know how an ancient Irish genealogy would have sounded. Bards memorised them as part of their repertoire and I imagine they would have been chanted, like whakapapa.

*Sheela-na-gig, p. 31.* There are 115 of the figures commonly called 'sheela-na-gig' recorded in Ireland. (And another fifty or so in Scotland and England.) The figures are a naked woman with a bony rib-cage and skull-like head and full voluptuous thighs spread wide in a crouch so that the vagina is very visible. Often the figure places her hands about her legs to draw the vagina open. They are found carved above church doors or windows and occasionally on castle walls.

Their history is obscure though they have formed part of ritual observance here for a very long time. They are often touched as part of a pilgrimage or for good fortune – at St Gobnait's shrine at Ballyvourney, for example, where a sheela-na-gig can be found near the church door. 'Sheela-na-gig' is not even necessarily their correct name: it was the name given to such a figure by a Tipperary farmer consulted during the Ordnance Survey of 1840. Spelled in Irish *Síle na gCíoch*, its precise meaning is unclear. 'Síle' means femininity but can also mean a woman with mysterious powers and is related to the word for a spirit.

'gCioch' means buttocks but 'gig' could also be related to 'gui', to pray. Other names were recorded for similar figures elsewhere: the 'Cailleach', for example, which is the Irish word used for both a nun – a woman in a Christian convent – and 'hag', meaning a woman possessed of pre-Christian spiritual powers. Which brings me to that old goddess of death and life, Hine-nui-te-Po and Maui trying to defeat death by crawling back into her vagina. And Te Rauparaha hiding in the kumara pit concealed by the old woman who sat above him with her cloak spread, and how he looked up and saw the place of origin, alluded to in the opening words of the great haka that now kicks off every All Black international.

*Betting, p. 33.* Three Spanish fishermen, according to *The Book of Invasions*, succeeded Cessair's band: 'a wright, a leech and a ruthless fisherman.'

*Gold, p. 35.* I hadn't expected the absolute perfection of the gold work, or the sheer quantity displayed in the main hall of the Irish National Museum. The gold is hammered so thin it is almost foil. There are several little cottonreel-shaped ornaments several centimetres in diameter, that were worn threaded through a distended ear lobe. Some contain little golden peas to rattle as the wearer walked.

I have read in a book about Danish bog burials the theory that the twisted form of the torque is possibly a stylised reference to the rope that was used in the ritual strangulation of victims sacrificed to the earth goddess in European bogs, just as a Christian wears a replica of the cross of the crucifixion.

*Rolling over, p. 36.* The limestone escarpment that reaches from Southland to Parnassus in North Canterbury is being exposed because the island is tipping gradually over. The most familiar account of the formation of New Zealand is the story of Maui fishing up the North Island while standing in the canoe that is the South Island. Last year I heard the Ngai Tahu account for the first time: that the island is the remains of Aoraki's great canoe, swamped by a massive wave and wrecked on a reef, its decorative prow the northern fjords, its broken pieces raked to one side in a heap by the god Tutaraki-whanua, to form the peninsula.

A geologist friend has told me that limestone is composed largely of the remains of bryozoa, who do indeed appear to die three times during their lifetimes, putrefying in their tiny shells before reviving and forming a new body. I was born in limestone country. My mother ate vegetables from our garden while I was in the womb. My bones are made from limestone. I contain the elements of creatures that have acquired the knack of resurrection. I like that.

*Ballad, p. 38.* In Cork 'quay' rhymes with 'away'. The central city occupies an island in the river and is ringed with former quays: the Coal Quay, the Potato Quay . . .

*Waving, p. 45.* Donoughmore means 'the great church', and is assumed to refer to the monastery founded here in the seventh century by the somewhat shadowy St Lachteen. Nothing remains of it today. The 'great church' now is up the road at Stuake, a trapezoidal construction opened in 1999 with blonde oak benches and a tower cut at an angle like the funnel on a Cunard liner.

The village feels curiously dispersed to a newcomer. There are two pubs at the crossroads, next door to each other – Pat Barrys and Sullys – but none of that cosy Gallic cluster of houses, shops, bakery, old forge and school around which the fields spread as from a nucleus. It is that distinctively Irish thing: a parish composed of many 'townlands', that fundamental unit of Irish settlement. The whole country is a complex jigsaw of over 62,000 townlands, some less than an acre, some more than a thousand acres in area, many consisting of a few farms and scattered houses and each knowing its own boundaries right enough, though these might not be especially evident to the outsider.

The arm bones of Donoughmore's patron saint were preserved in a yew box and placed inside an exquisitely worked reliquary of bronze and silver in about AD 1100. The finished work is small and slender and stands upright on the elbow with the fingers clenched in a fist. It was protected by the Healy family in Donoughmore for 500 years before being removed for reasons that remain unclear, quite probably by Jonathan Swift of Lilliput. In a mysterious fashion it then passed from hand to clerical hand before arriving in the National Museum soon after being displayed at the Great Exhibition of 1851.

John O'Connell, a local historian, tells me that when the church at Stuake was consecrated, the relic was brought down from Dublin. Great care was taken with its transport, of course, but for a brief period while an All-Ireland football final was on the TV at the pub, it was left to God's keeping.

Near the saint's arm in the museum are other treasures: fabulous crosiers and chalices, a tiny golden boat with frail oars, and woven textiles roughly stitched and rusty brown from their long concealment in some bog. By the exit stands a three-headed stone figure, each face oval, smooth-cheeked and mysterious – most probably an image of an old goddess in her customary triple manifestation.

*Well, p. 47.* At Castlemagner near Donoughmore, there is a holy well in the corner of a field with a figure who is listed as a sheela-na-gig but who bears little resemblance to the others. She is naked and carved in stone but she stands with her legs together, depicted from the knees up so that she seems to be rising from the earth and the long grass, and she has her arms raised like one of those Minoan snake goddesses.

She is still worshipped as St Brigit, and crosses have been crudely scratched on her torso and on the palms of her hands. She stands on one side of the well-cover which is made of stone and shaped like a beehive and covers just a small corner of her spring. The spring is broad and shallow, and covered with the circles caused by the bubbles rising through gravel. Above the central opening there is a kitchen cup on a little mantle and on the other side of the opening there is another stone that appears to be Roman, carved with a youth leaning upon one elbow with a cloak draped over one arm. It is probably some kind of funerary monument that has ended up here by some indirect route (for the Romans did not invade Ireland); something strange and of value in the corner of a lush field in Co. Cork.

*Rail, p. 49.* My father was born in Dundee where the family had lived since the middle of the nineteenth century, when the Irish flooded into Britain in such numbers that, by the 1860s, 25 per cent of the population in Liverpool, 18 per cent in Glasgow and 19 per cent in Dundee was Irish.

My grandfather was killed in France in 1918 in the last month of the First World War, and in 1920 my grandmother emigrated with her six children to New Zealand. She survived working as a cleaner for another six years before dying of emphysema when my father was fourteen.

He never set foot in Ireland, but he was intensely proud of being Irish. He read Irish history and fiction, sending away for books from Hodges Figgis in Dublin. He ordered two little heraldic shields too, to hang over the stereo, one for the Farrells, the other for his mother's family, the Slavens. (One had a hound with a broken chain leaping over a crown as its crest. He liked that especially.) He taught me how to write my name properly in Irish – Fionnaigh ni Fearghail – for the front of my school books. He swore in Irish. He sang, when drunk, the familiar repertoire of rebel songs. And when he died he was laid out in a kind of monk's habit. We hadn't expected that. It made him look foreign. 'The Irish shroud,' the undertaker explained to us. 'We don't often get asked for them any more.'

He remembered all his life seeing Ireland's coastline from the deck of the emigrant ship.

*Crop, p. 50.* The Lumper was a prolific potato that sustained millions of people in nineteenth-century Ireland. The Irish had taken some time to be persuaded of the potato's safety when it was first introduced in the seventeenth century, preferring their traditional diet of milk, barley and leeks. By the mid-nineteenth century, that diet had been displaced. The pig paid the rent, but it was the Lumper, with a little milk or butter, that supplied around 90 per cent of the daily diet of tenant families throughout the country. It was widely credited by observers with causing indolence, increasing fertility beyond sustainable levels and creating the delicate complexions of Irish women.

The Lumper, according to the Irish Seed Saver Catalogue, is a 'round/oval, knobbly white-skinned variety with deep eyes. Flesh is white and waxy but taste is poor and culinary use limited.' Nor does it keep very well, which meant that the summer months of June, July and August – the Hungry Months – were always particularly lean for poor families, even before the blight. The Lumper did have the advantage, however, of giving a good yield on poor soils. In form it sounds very similar to an old variety of potato that grows wild in the shingle in a rough little bay just around the headland from my home at Otanerito on Banks Peninsula, where the plants set tubers year after year among stones only a few metres from the surf.

The neighbour who showed me where they grow called them Maori potatoes: as kids they used to come here for picnics and boil them in a billy. They taste delicious, though they explode if boiled a few seconds too long: they're better baked or steamed in a hangi. Similar creamy, dimpled potatoes in the Koanga seed collection are named 'Whataroa'.

The description of the people sitting on their fences wailing for their ruined crop and the description of the 'typical Irish beggar' are both quoted from contemporary sources. The physical process of death by starvation is also as it was recorded by observers. A day or so before death, the body swelled to a deceptive plumpness. Then it burst.

*Lissadell, p. 52.*

> The light of evening, Lissadell,
> Great windows open to the south,
> Two girls in kimonos, both
> Beautiful, one a gazelle

Doug, who is my second husband, had copied these lines, along with 'The Wild Swans at Coole' and the lyrics to 'Mr Tambourine Man' into a folder when he headed off, aged eighteen, to hitch to Afghanistan back in 1973. He had packed the folder into a woven shoulder bag along with the other necessities – water bottle, t-shirt, a blanket. ('And underpants?' I prompt. Doug pauses. 'I don't recall any underpants,' he says.)

In early summer 2006, we visited Lissadell. And Coole. And Drumcliffe where Yeats lies buried.

It's a strange thing to visit a place because of a poem, to enter into collusion with some local Development Association busily promoting Yeats Country, to stop for a drink in the Yeats Tavern when the man himself entered a pub only once in his entire life.

The stories of Coole and Lissadell are, as it turns out, not primarily about Yeats at all, but about two of his associates: Lady Gregory, the playwright with whom he founded the Abbey Theatre; and one of the two girls drifting about in their kimonos, Constance Gore Booth, who as Constance Markiewicz took a leading role in the Easter Uprising. Like Yeats, both were members of the Anglo-Irish ascendancy born to privilege and an oppressive family history. Constance's grandfather, for example, had dispatched hundreds of tenants mid-century to New Brunswick to 'improve' his estate, including so many who were old or infirm that the colonial authorities objected to the nuisance. Both women devoted their lives to attempting to make amends for the wrongs of the past and to create a new and better Ireland.

The house at Coole was demolished in the 1950s, but you can visit the lake and woods and the autograph tree where the bark of the trunk is gradually growing over the initials carved by Synge and Shaw. The vast estate was redistributed as part of the new order, and the house abandoned after Lady Gregory's death: her daughter- in-law – 'a little suburban minx' according to Lily Yeats – did not like the place. As Lady Gregory lay dying of breast cancer in an upstairs bedroom, the minx had the living-room curtains taken down and rehung in her new house some miles away. The museum at Coole is in the former stables and tells its story through the words of one of Lady Gregory's granddaughters, who as children ran wild about the place and were banned from playing with the Yeats kids after they stuffed mud in their mouths.

At Lissadell the story is of an equally tempestuous child who in adulthood led a detachment of soldiers at St Stephen's Green during the muddle that was the Easter Uprising, and was observed taking potshots at members of the United Services Club which had windows overlooking the square. For this she was condemned to be executed but was rescued on account of her sex. She lived to be voted a seat at Westminster which she refused to take – though she did visit the Houses of Parliament incognito, just to see her name written by a coatpeg in the Members' cloakroom. When Ireland had its own Dáil she became a minister in the new cabinet, coping with the pragmatic realities of establishing a democratic state rather than the heroic utopia of the imagination.

Why did we go to Lissadell? Curiosity, I suppose. It was a wet day and it was in the tourist brochures. And what did we find there?

An unexpected empathy.

I am the descendant of Irish tenants, an illiterate scrum of Farrells, Slavens, Malones, O'Tooles and Dalys, that 'tribe of squalid apes' who fled to Scotland from starvation – yet I felt something curiously familiar in the stories of these women. Anglo-Irish, privileged, the inheritors of confiscated land: people I had been taught were the traditional enemy. Something about their love for a country their ancestors had invaded, something about the awkward excess of their attempts to come to terms with a complicated history.

But, most of all, we went to Lissadell because it is mentioned in a poem that a young man copied out into a green folder to carry along with a blanket, a t-shirt – and no underpants – to Afghanistan in 1973.

*Hunting, p. 53.* I like picking up local histories or turning off the road to visit strange local museums. (My favourite is the Benson and Hedges Fashion Award collection on the way to Naseby: that roomful of shoulder-padded and sequined trannie-glam in the middle of Central Otago.) I like little booklets with faded grey photographs of school children in rows, and victorious sports teams from the 1930s and the idiosyncratic recollections of local identities. I came across the hunting priest in such a history.

*The Battler, p. 55.* The oldest Irish book is called *An Cathach*, meaning 'The Battler', as it was used as a talisman in battle by the O'Donnells of Donegal. It has 58 pages and is a copy of the Psalms reputed to have been secretly copied by St Columba from a text owned by St Finian. When Finian objected to the plagiarism and the case was brought to court, the High King delivered a verdict in favour of Finian and the law of copyright: 'To every cow its calf, and to every book its copy.' The case led directly to a massive battle and to Columba's subsequent exile to Iona, where the little dove founded his monastery, sanctifying it first by burying one of his cousins alive.

Some time ago, I saw in a newspaper the instructions issued to the military operators responsible for firing cruise missiles: the instructions were in cartoon form.

*Poet, Novelist and above all Patriot, p. 56.* In New Zealand, the war memorial is at the centre of every community, with its column or pillar, its bronze soldier with bowed head, and its lists of the fallen from that area. There are often four sides to the plinth, one for the First World War, another for the Second. I always dislike the way there are often one or two sides still blank, as if they are waiting for the lists of dead from some upcoming military catastrophe: it's almost as if it has been planned for. I always read war memorials looking out for clusters of names and wondering about families who might have lost several sons, imagining the telegrams arriving and the distance between the place where their names are recorded, with its paddocks and magpies or its rows of shops and cars parked outside the SuperSave, and the places where they might lie buried. Northern France, Egypt, Cassino . . .

I began to notice soon after arriving in Ireland that the place where the war memorial would stand in New Zealand is often occupied by a bronze statue of a writer. In the middle of Mallow where I sometimes go to do the shopping, there is a statue of John Joseph Fitzgerald, Scholar and Champion of All Oppressed. Outside the castle in Limerick there is a statue of a man, not on horseback wielding a sword, but holding an open book: Michael Hogan, 'the Bard of Thomond', along with an extract from his *Lays and Legends of Thomond*:

> I never learned a common rule in any book
> For I like every headstrong fool
> My own way took . . .

At the head of the main street in Ennistymon is the seated figure of Brian Merriman, author of *The Midnight Court*, while Tipperary is under the protection of Charles J. Kickham, 'Poet, Novelist and above all Patriot'.

There are sometimes war memorials too, but they are different from the ones at home. They remember men who fought during the First World War – though not the Second, 'The Emergency', when Ireland remained neutral. Or Irish-born generals – like Wellington – or battles in the Crimea, when the British army had a large Irish component (around 40 per cent of the infantry throughout the nineteenth century were Irish men). Roadside memorials recall the deaths of men in ambushes or battles during the 1920s. The area of Ireland around Donoughmore saw fierce fighting between the Irish and the Black and Tans: parts of Cork city were burned to the ground and two of the city's mayors died. Thomas MacCurtain was murdered, while his successor, Terence MacSwiney, died after a 74-day hunger strike in Brixton Prison.

Later fighting, between Irish supporters of the Treaty which divided Ireland into its current form and those who wanted a united Ireland, was

89

bitter as only civil wars can be. The memorials are everywhere, sometimes marked by nothing more than a plaque on a stone wall, sometimes with flag and massive marble plinth among the rocks and heather.

The Celts, according to the Roman writer Tacitus, were roused for battle against the Romans by druidic women dressed in 'black attire like the Furies, with hair dishevelled, waving brands' who ran shrieking and chanting between the ranks of men.

*The brown bull, p. 57.* The first cattle in the South Island were brought ashore and farmed around the bay where I live, Otanerito on Banks Peninsula. Dense forest was cleared for their pasture.

*The flood, p. 59.* When the River Lee was dammed near Macroom, it drowned part of a vast inland delta of streams and little islands called the Gearagh. Farms disappeared beneath the water, just as valleys vanished when the dam at Benmore was built in the 1950s. Before construction began, the Oamaru Power Board where my father worked took employees and their families for a bus trip to the site and back via Omarama. Years later, I read Buddy Mikaere's book *Te Maiharoa and the Promised Land* and that whole landscape took on other layers of meaning: not just pubs and dams and sheep farms, but a history of people driven from their homes who set off, led by a prophet, in search of secure territory in this valley and of the events that occurred along the way. Like the moment when an express train was stopped in its tracks by the prophet, to permit his people to cross the combined rail and road bridge over the Waitaki in their wagons, without coming to harm. An old woman recalled seeing the engine's wheels spinning on the spot as they passed over.

*Road, p. 61.* The landscape of Ireland is like the New Zealand landscape in that it is not always easy to read. It's not always grandly signposted. The stories often lie in the detail. In a field near us in Donoughmore, for example, there is a kind of embankment that runs along the fenceline for a few hundred metres before ending in a hillside. You'd miss it if you did not know what to look for.

It's a famine road.

There are dozens of them throughout Ireland. Unable ideologically to simply dispense charity, local landowners paid men to build walls around their properties (there are miles of famine walls – beautifully built by skilled stone workers – throughout Ireland and also ringing properties in England and Scotland). Or they engaged gangs of men to build lengths of road. This work could not compete with established business, nor

90

could it have any commercial value. So the roads simply begin, then end arbitrarily.

Near the famine road, which is now overgrown with pine trees, the real road broadens slightly by a gate. It's not named on a map but it was the site of a settlement where people lived under whatever shelter they could improvise. It's noticeable that there are relatively few old cottages in Ireland: that's because a lot of people lived in temporary structures of mud or stone; eighteenth-century visitors describe Irish families living in ox-hide tents. And the traces of such structures disappear.

*Hair, p. 63.* My younger daughter wears her hair in long waist-length dreadlocks. She took a holiday from her job on Anchor Island off the coast of Fiordland, where she works caring for some of the last 83 kakapo in existence, to spend a month with me in Ireland. Her hair caused a bit of a stir. It's a common enough hair-style in New Zealand but not in Ireland – at least not in 2006. It was fashionable a couple of millennia ago, however: the Celts evidently admired red-blonde hair so thickly matted that the wearer would not feel an apple fall into it. Cúchulainn, for example, is described as having hair dyed in three colours – dark at the roots, brown in the middle and fair at the tips – and tangled 'like the hawthorne branches used to refence a gap in a hedge'.

*The Hag of Beare, p. 64.* When you come from a country where wood has been the traditional material used for building and there are still areas of primeval forest, the stoniness of Ireland is striking. It takes a while to adjust to stone walls, stone buildings, bare stone where forest was cleared so long ago that the bare bones feel like the natural cover.

Then there are the stones that have been accorded special reverence. Stones that have been adapted by human hands – such as the Turoe Stone with its carved tendrils bursting from a kind of basketweave like a bouquet in stone, dating from around the third century BC. It stood for centuries on an Iron Age hill fort until the nineteenth century when it was moved to the lowlands. Today you find it housed in a wooden garden shed on a manicured lawn at a pet farm occupied by ducklings and piglets and excited three-year-olds. The shed is necessary because the carvings that had survived on a hillside for centuries are fading rapidly.

I especially like the stones that have not been adapted but which are held in regard for themselves alone, like the erratic which in the fifth century supposedly floated on to the foreshore at Ardmore bearing St Declan's bell and vestments over the sea from Wales. It cures backache, if you can crawl beneath it through the narrow gap where it stands balanced on razor-sharp ridges of rock that are under water at high tide.

91

I considered it – but I don't suffer from a bad back and it would have totally destroyed my jeans.

The Hag of Beare is the name given to a rounded boulder about a metre and half high that stands on a promontory facing the sea near Eyeries on the Beara Peninsula. It is creviced and bubbly: a solitary volcanic erratic among acres of smooth-cheeked granite. Viewed from certain angles it has something of the air of a small fat woman crouched upon her haunches. There is no fuss: no carpark, just a little wooden sign on the fence, but the track through the bracken is well trodden and there are coins and hairclips laid on her crevices.

*The Lament of the Nun of Beare, p. 65.* I don't know how stone and verse might be connected, if at all – but the Hag of Beare turns up again as the speaker in the most famous and powerful of all Old Irish poems, 'The Lament of the Hag / Nun / Old Woman' – take your pick to translate 'Cailleach' – 'of Beare'.

The author is unknown. It was first written down in the tenth century, but it was probably composed much earlier, in the fifth or sixth century at the time when Christianity was displacing the old religion.

It's an amazing poem: a howl of protest, a storm of grief from an old woman who has lived in her youth as a pagan priestess, but must now adjust to living as a nun under the new Christian religious regime. I love its physicality – the blood in the first stanza (today she'd no doubt be a candidate for HRT), the vision of the young woman in bright clothing driving across a plain in her chariot, the present desolation of storm and an empty house, the linking of tide and body and life. I love the way she yells down the centuries from her hut by the sea, objecting to the new world order.

My version of the lament is rough. I don't read Old Irish so it is based on a literal English translation in *The Golden Treasury of Irish Verse*. That also uses quatrains, but I can tell, looking at lines I don't understand, that I haven't come anywhere close to the rhythmic and rhyming complexity of the original, and I'll inevitably have missed all sorts of delicate cross referencing. But it's as near as I can get to her.

*Dance, p. 69.* Irish set dancing is small and intricate, designed to be danced in a crowded cottage kitchen without knocking into the dresser. A friend who teaches mathematics in the computer department at University College Cork took us to our first céilidh. It was held in a small corrugated-iron hall near Blarney. I was in the lobby when the dancing began: suddenly eighty pairs of feet began beating the floor in exact rhythm. It was like being inside a kettle drum.

The patterns shifted rapidly in sequences of repetition and variation which the dancers knew without being prompted by a caller. A single accordion provided the music but it could scarcely be heard above the tattoo of dancing feet. As a child we used to dance about the living room to Jimmy Shand and his band. But Scottish dance music sounds four square by comparison. There is a one two three four-ness about it. It observes bar lines. Irish dance music leaves no room for pause: it is seamless, breathless, unfurling as the exact aural equivalent of the curvilinear pattern in an ornamented book. It's a classical form, depending upon the deliberate restraining of possibility for its effects. The dances employed a tightly limited repertoire of movements to create different patterns, and in the poem, I've tried to imitate that: same words, different sequence, different meaning.

*Bed, p. 71.* Irish bards, both men and women, learned their craft in schools where a large part of the curriculum involved lying in the dark on their beds committing law, genealogy and history to memory and composing poetry. While we were in Ireland, an elderly member of the family spent some time in hospital where, under the influence of various painkillers, he watched brilliantly coloured movies of his life.

One classic form of Irish poetry requires a seven-syllable line, a caesura at the fifth syllable, and that the first word of the first line must be repeated as the final word of the last line. I like the way that last detail suggests the same aesthetic – the same recognition of when a pattern is complete – as the curvilinear design that has a dragon twisting and bending over a surface until it ends by eating its own tail.

*The verb 'to be', p. 72.* When my younger daughter came to visit me in Ireland, we walked up all the high hills.

We climbed Mount Brandon from the glaciated valley on the eastern side, on one of those days that are half sun, half swirling fog. At the crest there is a spring and the ruins of chapels. I was nervous in the fog but my daughter is used to much wilder places. 'We'll be right,' she said. 'There's a track.'

We climbed Croagh Patrick, up the slippery path from the enormous carpark and visitor centre, to the crest where the fog was thick and the chapel was closed and a chill wind tore at the flimsy remnants of shelters built to give some protection to the thousands who come here each year. Toward the top we met a man who was climbing using a *camán* ( the stick used in hurling or the women's version of the game, *camogie*) as a support on the stony ground. Players balance the ball – the *sliotar* – on the head of the *camán*, running with it as we used to run races carrying an egg on a dessert spoon. The man showed us some names written on the head of the *camán*. 'You'll recognise these,' he said. We didn't and felt awkward at not knowing: an All-Ireland champion *camogie* team he had coached, his daughter's name among them. Some time after their victory, when she was lying ill in hospital, he had made a vow to climb Croagh Patrick thirty times if only she could be made well. He carried the *camán* each time. This was his twenty-ninth pilgrimage.

We climbed Errigal, a steep-sided peak like Taranaki in Donegal. Irish is still spoken round here and the man who ran the hostel was passionate for the language. It is subtle, he said. There are, for instance, two verbs meaning 'to be': one suggests permanence ('this is the floor'); the other suggests transience, and is used, for example, when speaking of the weather ('it is sunny'). I like that distinction.

I walked up the tracks behind my daughter, with her strong legs, her bobbing hair. Not that long ago, I led her. I can still feel the weight of her, carrying her when she didn't want to walk any more, between banks of tussocks and flowering hebes on the track at Tongariro or through the bearded bush at Dawson Falls or on some sunny Sunday walk near Pohangina: the feel of her little duffel coat and her red tights and her feathery hair, usually chopped into a jagged fringe by herself using the toenail scissors. Now she takes the lead and I'm following and, behind us, there's that long queue of people stretching back down into the fog.

*Daffodils, p. 74.* 'Otanerito' is the name of the bay where I live on Banks Peninsula. 'O tane' – of the man. And 'rito', the tight sheath of new leaf at the centre of a flax plant. The bay is notable for the tall phallic rock stack at its entrance that whalers named Pompey's Pillar. They called the bay itself 'Long Bay', one of three 'Long Bays' on the peninsula. (Whalers do not seem to have been an especially imaginative lot.) But the map's been changed and now the bay is known as Otanerito: the growing point of a man.

Behind our house the previous owners had spelled out 'Long Bay' in daffodils across the steep hillside. The flowers come up every spring, growing more blurred and chaotic by the year as the plants multiply. It's hard to make out the individual letters now.

In Ireland names have also gone through many changes, in particular when map makers and administrators altered the original Irish to an Anglicised version that frequently obscures the meaning.

Names shift with successive invasions.

The land survives.